Safari Sam's Wild Animals

Jungle Animals

A+

Smart Apple Media

Published by Smart Apple Media, an imprint of Black Rabbit Books
P.O. Box 3263, Mankato, Minnesota 56002
www.smartapplemedia.com

Produced by David West Children's Books
6 Princeton Court, 55 Felsham Road, London SW15 1AZ

Designed and illustrated by David West

Copyright © 2014 David West Children's Books

Cataloging-in-Publication Data is available from
Library of Congress
ISBN 978-1-62588-072-7

Printed in China
CPSIA compliance information: DWCB15CP
311214

9 8 7 6 5 4 3 2 1

Safari Sam says:
I will tell you something
more about the animal.

Learn what this
animal eats.

Where in the
world is the
animal found?

Its size is revealed!

What animal group
is it—mammal, bird,
reptile, amphibian,
insect, or something
else?

Interesting facts.

Contents

Black Panthers

Black panthers are one of the top **predators** in the jungle. Their dark fur is ideal **camouflage** in the forest's shadows as they stalk their **prey**. Black leopards are found in Asia. Black jaguars live in South America.

Safari Sam says:
Cougars, leopards, and jaguars are all sometimes called panthers. When leopards and jaguars have the unusual black skin and fur coloring, they are called black panthers.

Black leopard

Black panthers eat meat. Their prey varies from birds and fish to mammals and reptiles.

Black panthers are found in the jungles of Asia and South America.

Leopards have a body length of about 7.5 feet (2 meters).

Panthers are mammals. Mammals have fur and give birth to live young.

A black jaguar mated with a lioness, who then gave birth to a black jaglion.

5

Safari Sam says:
Female boa constrictors can give birth to as many as 60 live babies at a time. They start life at 2 feet (0.6 meters) long and grow continually throughout their 25- to 30-year lives.

Boa constrictors will eat anything they can catch and fit into their mouths, including birds, bats, monkeys, and rodents.

Boa constrictor

Boa Constrictors

The boa constrictor is a large snake that captures its prey with its jaws. The boa quickly wraps its body around its victim and squeezes it until it suffocates. Its jaws can stretch wide to swallow medium-to-large-sized prey whole. After this meal, the snake might not eat for several months.

Boa constrictors are found in tropical Central and South America.

Boa constrictors can grow from 10 to 14 feet (3 to 4.3 meters) long and can weigh more than 60 pounds (27 kilograms).

Boa constrictors are reptiles and members of the boa snake family.

The largest boa constrictor ever measured was 18 feet (5.5 meters) long.

Chameleons

These strange-looking lizards come in a variety of sizes and colors. Their eyes can rotate and focus separately to observe two different objects at the same time. They capture prey by firing out their long, sticky-tipped tongues.

8

Panther chameleon

Chameleons are mainly insectivores, which means they only eat insects, but some also will eat snails, worms, lizards, amphibians, and plant material.

Chameleons inhabit tropical and mountain rain forests, savannahs, and sometimes deserts in Africa, Madagascar, the Middle East, southern Europe, and southern Asia. They have also been introduced to Hawaii, California, and Florida.

Panther chameleons can grow up to 10 inches (23 centimeters) in length.

Chameleons are reptiles.

Chameleons are able to change their skin color. They do this to signal to each other, as well as to blend in with their surroundings.

Chimpanzees are mostly fruit and plant eaters, but they also feed on insects, eggs, and meat.

Chimpanzees live in African jungles, woodlands, and grasslands.

Chimpanzees grow up to 5.5 feet (1.7 meters) in height and can weigh up to 130 pounds (59 kilograms).

Chimpanzees are mammals and members of the primate order, which also includes humans.

Although they normally walk on all fours, chimpanzees can also stand and walk upright.

Chimpanzees

Chimpanzees spend much of their time in trees. They can quickly travel through the leafy jungle canopy by swinging from branch to branch. At night, they sleep in tree-top nests made from branches and leaves.

Safari Sam says:
Chimpanzees are one of the few animals that use tools. They use sticks to get to insects in their nests and can crack open nuts with stones.

Chimpanzee

11

Safari Sam says:
Like chimpanzees, gorillas use tools for different tasks. One gorilla has been seen testing the depth of a swamp with a stick before wading through it.

Gorilla

Gorillas usually eat fruit, plant shoots, and leaves. Occasionally, they eat ants and termites.

Gorillas live in jungles in Africa.

Wild male gorillas can grow to 6 feet (1.8 meters) tall and weigh up to 400 pounds (180 kilograms).

Gorillas are mammals and members of the primate order.

The silverback gorilla protects the members of the troop from predators, such as leopards.

Gorillas

Gorillas live in groups, called troops, led by a large male called a silverback. The leader is named for the silver hair that grows on his back when he is about 12 years of age. The troop divides the day between eating, resting, and moving to feeding grounds.

13

African forest elephant

African forest
elephants feed on
grass, leaves, bark,
fruit, and other
vegetation.

Safari Sam says:
African forest elephants talk to each
other using noises. They use low calls
that can be heard by other elephants
several miles away. These sounds are
too low to be heard by people.

14

Jungle Elephants

African elephants have no natural predators. They use their trunk to touch and to hold objects and food. The trunk can suck up water for drinking and spraying on their bodies.

African forest elephants are found in the lowland jungles of west and central Africa.

Male African forest elephants can grow to 11 feet (3.4 meters) in length and weigh about 6 tons (5 metric tons).

Elephants are mammals.

African forest elephants can drink up to 40 gallons (150 liters) of water in one day.

Orangutans

Like gorillas and chimpanzees, orangutans are members of the great ape family. They spend most of their time alone, feeding on fruit in the trees. Young orangutans stay with their mothers for two years before they start to move around on their own. From the age of two, they may travel holding hands with an older orangutan.

Safari Sam says:
The name "orangutan" comes from the Malay and Indonesian words "orang," meaning "person," and "hutan," meaning "forest." From these definitions, the name "orangutan" means "person of the forest."

Baby orangutan

Orangutans mainly eat fruit, but will also eat vegetation, bark, honey, insects, and even bird eggs.

Orangutans are found only in the rain forests of Borneo and Sumatra.

Larger male orangutans can stand about 4.5 feet (1.4 meters) tall and weigh about 180 pounds (80 kilograms).

Orangutans are mammals and members of the primate order.

Orangutans make several different types of calls and have been known to **blow a raspberry!**

17

Safari Sam says:
Parrots, along with the crow family of birds, are among the most intelligent birds. Some **species** can imitate human voices.

Red-and-green macaw

18

Most parrots eat seeds, nuts, fruit, buds, and other plant material.

Parrots are found in Central and South America, Africa, South Asia, and Australasia.

The wingspan of the red-and-green macaw can be up to 49 inches (125 centimeters), with a total body length of 37 inches (94 centimeters).

Parrots are birds, which are feathered, two-legged, and lay eggs.

Macaws and some other parrots often eat clay from riverbanks. The clay is rich in **sodium,** which the parrots need to stay healthy.

Parrots

Parrots vary in size from small pygmies to large macaws. Many parrots use their feet to hold nuts while they crack the nuts open with their hooked beaks. Most parrots nest in hollows in trees or in cavities dug into cliffs, banks, or the ground.

19

Poison Dart Frogs

These brightly colored frogs are highly poisonous. They are called "dart frogs" because local tribespeople put the frogs' poison on the tips of their blowdarts. Then, they fire the darts through long blowpipes at prey, such as monkeys.

Poison dart frogs feed on all types of insects.

Poison dart frogs can be found in the jungles of Central and South America.

Most poison dart frogs are very small, less than 0.59 inches (1.5 centimeters) in length, although a few can grow to 2.4 inches (6.1 centimeters) long.

Poison dart frogs are amphibians, which can live in and out of water.

Adult frogs lay their eggs in moist places. Once the eggs hatch, the adult piggybacks the tadpoles, one at a time, to a pool of water.

Safari Sam says:
Poison dart frogs are brightly colored to warn off predators. This method works for some other species of frog that are not poisonous!

Poison dart frog

21

Tigers

Tigers live a solitary life and are excellent hunters. Tigers use their striped coat to camouflage themselves and ambush their prey from the jungle shadows. They are strong swimmers and enjoy cooling off in ponds, lakes, and rivers.

Tigers mostly feed on large- and medium-sized animals, such as water buffalo, small deer, and wild boar.

Tigers are an endangered species and can be found only in Asia.

Tigers grow to 8 or 9 feet (2 or 3 meters) long and weigh about 300 to 400 pounds (150 to 200 kilograms).

Tigers are mammals and members of the cat family.

A tiger can survive up to one week without eating, but then it can eat up to 90 pounds (40 kilograms) of food in one meal.

Tiger

Safari Sam says:
Tigers can be different colors. White tigers and golden tigers have been seen in the wild.

23

Glossary

blow a raspberry
To stick out your tongue and blow to make a funny sound.

camouflage
Colors or patterns on an animal's body that help it to blend with its surroundings.

predator
An animal that hunts other animals for food.

prey
An animal that is hunted by another for food.

sodium
An essential mineral for many animals' diets.

species
A group of animals that have similar characteristics and can produce offspring.

Index